IMAGES
of America

ORANGE PARK

IMAGES
of America

ORANGE PARK

Cynthia Cheatwood

ARCADIA
PUBLISHING

Published by Arcadia Publishing
Charleston, South Carolina

Printed in the United States of America

Library of Congress Control Number: 2020930359

For all general information, please contact Arcadia Publishing:
Telephone 843-853-2070
Fax 843-853-0044
E-mail sales@arcadiapublishing.com
For customer service and orders:
Toll-Free 1-888-313-2665

Visit us on the Internet at www.arcadiapublishing.com

CONTENTS

ACKNOWLEDGMENTS

This book has been generations in the making. I am indebted to all the local historians of the town of Orange Park. Every iconic photograph, every dictated story, every oral history, photograph album, and recorded memory has woven a charm into the history of Orange Park that is symbolic of American ideals and human foibles. My humble efforts to compile these into a chronological picture would have failed without the assistance of certain individuals.

Mary Jo McTammany, a true guardian of Orange Park memories, has been a vital help in this project. Her insights and clarity helped clear up subtle misconnects along my way. She shared treasured rare photographs for this book, a fact I consider the greatest demonstration of the importance of telling these stories.

I appreciate the assistance of Vishi Garig, Clay County's archives specialist, and the willingness of current and past town representatives to contribute images and ideas. The unflagging support of my fellow members of the Historical Society of Orange Park has kept me on track and energized. I appreciate Carolyn and Barney Clark, Steve Howard, and Van Hogan, in particular, for setting other things aside to help make this book possible. Finally, I acknowledge the patience of my husband, Richard Cheatwood, who lost me for days on end as I puzzled through over 14 decades of personalities.

Images for this book have been shared through a few main sources, which are abbreviated as follows: Clay County Archives (CCA), Historical Society of Orange Park (HSOP), Town of Orange Park (TOP), and State Archives of Florida (SAF).

INTRODUCTION

Harriet Beecher Stowe, who lived a short while in Orange Park before its township, wrote fondly, "The land is unusually good, beautifully situated on the river with fine bluffs and a clear shore." She had been drawn to Orange Park, like generations after her, by the promise of better health in the Florida sunshine. A street in town still bears her name.

The history of Orange Park is tied to the land, as Stowe described it. From the Timucua people who occupied the area starting 1,300 years ago to residents today, the riverfront community has offered abundant access to water resources, fertile soil, mild climate, and quiet greenspaces that nurture both body and soul.

In 1939, botanist Ada Yerkes wrote, "The St. John's River, apart from its natural beauty, sunshine and moonlight dancing on its surface . . . links one to the past and stirs one's imagination as to men and events of long ago." Writing from its Orange Park banks, she added, "History has passed this way, has rushed or dawdled with varying footsteps." That history will be presented in this book as an homage to all who made the town what it is today.

When white settlers moved into the area, it was the land and water they wanted. As Americans were declaring independence in 1776, a 2,600-acre British plantation, Laurel Grove, was established by Loyalists William and Rebecca Pengree. They grew cotton and citrus with slave labor until forced to leave Laurel Grove during the British evacuation that followed the American Revolution. They settled in Georgia, but Creek hostilities persuaded William to return to his plantation in 1786 with his wife, child, and 48 slaves. The Spanish granted them their land in return for naval stores produced with Pengree's water-powered sawmill. Laurel Grove, with its plentiful trees, was a great provider of turpentine, tar, and pitch, important for Spanish ships.

Shortly after their return, however, William Pengree died, leaving Rebecca to manage the plantation. She sold the property to Zephaniah Kingsley in 1803 and moved back to Georgia. Kingsley swore an oath of allegiance to Spain and purchased more land along Doctors Lake, bringing in 100 slaves. He planted 700 mandarin orange trees to stand behind a 2,000-foot "bearing orange hedge." Native concerns led him to install a 12-foot-high, hand-hewn cypress picket fence around the whole orange grove. He ambitiously acquired even more land throughout northeast Florida.

Kingsley developed Laurel Grove further with help from his Senegalese wife, Anna Madgigine Jai. Captured and forced into slavery at a young age, Anna was sold to Kingsley in the Caribbean when she was 13 years old. He was a West Indies merchant and ship captain, as well as a slave master, spending much of his time away from Laurel Grove. Over time, he grew more and more reliant on Anna, who had proven herself to be a shrewd and practical woman, able to handle the day-to-day business of the plantation. She learned to maximize the value of each field, each crop, even each slave under her watch. Kingsley manumitted her in 1811, when she was 18 years old. Over the next few years, he presented her with land and slaves of her own, which she administered along with Laurel Grove.

Also in 1811, James Madison and his secretary of state, James Monroe, plotted to invade Spanish East Florida to make it a new territory of the United States. Congress passed a secret act to initiate the action. Georgia governor Gen. George Mathews led soldiers into Florida under the precept that US forces must support local revolts against the Spanish. By March 1812, the Patriots, as they called themselves, came into Florida with the US Navy and Georgia's John McIntosh, who had taken command after Matthew's death by natural causes. They took possession of Fernandina and Amelia Island, but soon thereafter, Madison changed his mind and reversed his decision, saying the action was a bad idea.

All along the St. Johns River, large plantation owners were coerced into joining the Patriots Rebellion. The only other option they had was to be burned out by McIntosh's militia, so many complied, including Zephaniah Kingsley. For a time, Laurel Grove was actually the capital of the Patriots' "Republic of East Florida."

As the United States was declaring war on Great Britain, Native forces were joining the Spanish against the Patriots. The whole enterprise became very unorganized and frenzied. While tensions escalated, Zephaniah Kingsley continued his sea trade, and when Laurel Grove was on the brink of attack, he was far out at sea. Anna alone had to save what could be secured, especially the plantation's slaves.

American takeover would mean slavery again for Anna and her children. She plotted with a Spanish gunboat captain, secured her "people," and made sure Laurel Grove would not fall into Patriot hands. She set a slow burn to ignite a cannon in the main house at just the right moment. She and her people were safe on the waiting Spanish gunboat when the house exploded around the marauding invaders. She took her family and slaves to Fernandina and then Fort George Island, where the family would establish Kingsley Plantation, now a national park site.

In an interesting twist, the land that Kingsley went on to develop on Fort George Island was once owned by the same John McIntosh who led the Patriots Rebellion. As the door closed on annexing Florida, McIntosh bought Laurel Grove and rebuilt it into a thriving plantation. The fertility of the land proved itself once again. McIntosh developed the land so well that by the time of his death in 1836, his sugar mill and sawmill operations had made him the largest slave owner in the area.

In 1845, Florida became a state, and in 1858, Clay County split out of Duval County. More people, especially northerners, were falling in love with the area. When the Civil War raged in the 1860s, Laurel Grove began to fade. Ownership changed hands, from McIntosh to Stephen Bryan in 1852 and then in 1863 to Catherine Hookey of Georgia, who owned it during the war years.

The lure of the river, the abundance of undeveloped land, and the clean temperate air—all of these lured Washington Gano Benedict to the St. Johns River. In 1876, this enterprising Bostonian purchased 9,000 acres that included Laurel Grove Plantation. He and associates such as Alpheus Blake and David Loring formed the Florida Winter Home and Improvement Corporation with hopes of monopolizing on the land's productivity.

Benedict laid out streets with farm and home lots, each planted with orange trees to entice northern investors. He built a large hotel with a 1,400-foot dock for steamboat traffic. In a flurry of activity, he published advertising pamphlets and newspaper ads, formed a few local businesses, and laid out a 200-foot sign facing the river with the words "Orange Park" in letters large enough to be read by passing river traffic. He went so far as to go to the docks in Jacksonville, where settlers or tourists might disembark, and loudly proclaim the charms of Orange Park, persuading many to skip Jacksonville in favor of his hotel, the Magnetic Roaring Springs nearby, and even the novelty of Indian mounds within a short walk from the dock.

The enterprise was a success. Benedict was able to sell most of the available lots and to encourage some high-society folks to visit Orange Park. President Grant and Philip Sheridan, with their wives, visited in 1880. Other notables came to the area, including William Astor, who helped in the creation of Grace Episcopal Church. B.J. Johnson came in the 1880s, establishing the Winterbourne estate. They spent winters at Benedict's grand hotel, which existed under many names throughout its history. Dances and other social events at the hotel often included invitations to local residents. Benedict, hoping to present an image of lively capacity, was known to ride through town on horseback, inviting locals to join the festivities.

The Jacksonville, Tampa & Key West Railroad began to run through Orange Park in 1884. The 10 stops it made between Orange Park and Palatka during that two-and-a-half-hour ride were in tiny towns, most of which no longer exist. The farther they sat from the vital St. Johns River, the less likely they were to survive.

In 1890, a school was established with the goal of educating African Americans. Begun by the American Missionary Association, the school was sponsored by Daniel Hand and stressed the importance of skills education as well as academics. The school produced teachers to expand its mission. There were conflicts with the school from local white neighbors, and it ceased to function in 1917 after years of racial challenges.

Settling families started making improvements to the town. William and Carrie Kellogg Clarke moved to the area from Jacksonville. William ran a successful plumbing business there but wanted his son to have a more rural boyhood. He purchased 30 acres in 1910, starting a profitable pecan grove; he built the family home, which is now owned by the town, around 1912. To travel to and from the plumbing business, he had a choice to drive or go by steamboat. The *May Garner* steamboat made regular stops in Orange Park, Green Cove Springs, Mandarin, and Jacksonville, transporting everything the town required, including crops, mail, and people. William became mayor, and his wife was a member of several organizations in the town. The Clarkes were always generous with neighbors, offering the use of their home and resources.

Leonidas Wade, a local attorney and businessman, bought land on Doctors Lake, just southwest of the new town limits. The area, which had gone by several names, was generally referred to as Seminole Springs. Wade changed the name to Wadesboro Springs and sold bottled water from the springs to people in St. Augustine, where the natural water had a sulfur taste. This helped to stimulate the local economy. The water was even said to have been sent to the president at the White House.

The St. Johns River, which defines Orange Park's eastern border, and Doctors Lake to its south continued to provide. Fishing was an occupation for many in Orange Park. In 1914, the Carnes Fish Camp opened on Doctors Lake with hundreds of lines cast nightly to catch fish to be sold in Jacksonville. Each morning, boats pulled up to the Carnes dock to unload the night's haul. The fish were beheaded, weighed, packed in boxes with ice and moss, and bound for Jacksonville to be shipped far and wide.

By the 1920s, the old sawmill days were passing, but the area trees continued to give. Naval stores became the backbone of the local economy. African American workers came to the area to work in the turpentine industry, on farms, and for the burgeoning railroad. These jobs were important, because oranges were less practical after winter freezes of the 1890s. In 1921, the Loyal Order of the Moose purchased a large piece of the town to create "the City of Contentment" (now Moosehaven) for its retiring members.

Caleb and Elinor Johnson, heirs of B.J. Johnson, built a Mediterranean Revival luxury estate, Mira Rio, in 1922 on property adjacent to Winterbourne. This opulent addition to the riverfront brought upscale attention to Orange Park. Guests arrived by yacht, and many jobs were created to maintain the house and grounds. During World War II, using the name Azaleana Manor, rooms would be leased to men in training for Air Force leadership at nearby military bases.

In 1923, the growth of local crops led to the creation of a new road for trucks to transport produce. Electricity followed the next year. The Woman's Club (established in 1910), which contributed significantly to the quality of life in town, built a meeting place in 1929; it still stands. The year 1930 saw the opening of the Yale Laboratories of Primate Biology in Orange Park, studying behaviors of chimpanzees. Dr. Robert Yerkes conducted the first detailed observations of chimpanzee development and reproductive processes at this facility. The thick woods and warm climate provided a natural environment similar to that of Africa. It was nicknamed "the Monkey Farm" by locals, who have many stories of experiences with the local chimps. The research center closed in 1965, but the work continues still at Emory University.

Greyhound racing began at the Clay County Kennel Club in 1931 and continued later as the Orange Park Kennel Club. Little changed for years thereafter. Civic organizations began to develop. The Garden Club of Orange Park began in the late 1940s, motivated to make the town more attractive. The Clothes Closet and Food Pantry, originally the Church Women's Christian Ministries, began serving the community in 1952 by providing emergency assistance with food, clothing, household, and financial needs.

In 1946, things changed, as Telfair Stockton developed a large tract of land for a neighborhood named Holly Point. This land was converted to upscale housing for families that wanted waterfront at a reasonable cost. At the same time, an elegant harness racing facility opened for a short but noteworthy time on Wells Road. A decade later, architect Robert Broward designed a style of homes that today is called mid-century modern, a ranch layout with large glass windows on the back and privacy features. Orange Park became the focus of resettlement from Duval County, earning it the status of Jacksonville's bedroom community. The Buckman Bridge was opened in 1974 to connect them, proving so important that it had to be expanded in 1997.

Many people lived their whole lives within the small boundaries of Orange Park. Proximity to Naval Air Station Jacksonville has also meant many people lived here for only a few years. A gathering of townspeople would reveal that a large number are second-generation military transplants.

The history of the town is cherished by its old-timers but less known to newer folks. In 2003, a group of citizens got together and formed the Historical Society of Orange Park to keep memories alive. Their efforts helped preserve the historic Clarke House, which is now a public treasure. In 2011, the society, with the inspiration and dedication of Carolyn Anne Day, created the Veterans Memorial at Magnolia Cemetery. This project was cosponsored with the Daughters of the American Revolution, Town of Orange Park, and American Legion Riders No. 250.

Today, land along Orange Park's historic riverfront is at a premium. The schools are good, and the people are friendly. Town parks provide popular greenspaces for fun and relaxation. Public events bring out thousands to share old-fashioned fellowship. The Orange Park Athletic Association and Orange Park Skateboard Park offer young people the opportunity for fun in the sunshine. The lure of natural beauty, location, and resources that inspired Stowe, Benedict, Dr. Yerkes, and countless others still beckons.

One

THE FIRST
HUNDRED YEARS

The area now designated as "the Springs" in Orange Park has watched the town's history unfold. From the Native Timucua people over 1,300 years ago to town citizens today, these springs have served many purposes. The water bubbles up from the sand and soil before traveling under a footbridge and out into the St. Johns River to witness canoes, steamboats, yachts, good times and bad, and generations of Americans. (HSOP.)

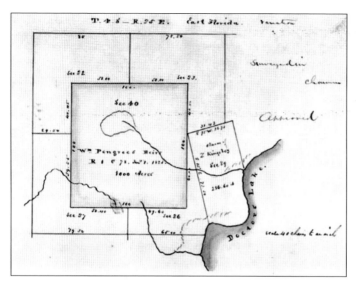

The first European claims for the land that makes up Orange Park were granted by the British in 1766 to Sir John Perceval, who saw the potential for British plantations in Florida. The original grantee, James Crisp, never actually came to the area he had prepared for development. Instead, it was settled by Loyalists William and Rebecca Pengree in 1776. They named their 2,600 acres Laurel Grove Plantation. (SAF.)

The Pengrees were forced out of Florida when the Spanish regained control in 1783 but were permitted to return in 1786 after promising to use their sawmill to help produce Spanish naval stores. During Wagner's War in 1794, the Pengrees lost much to warring Natives, and William Pengree died shortly afterwards. Rebecca could not continue without him. So, in 1803, Laurel Grove Plantation was sold to slave-trader Zephaniah Kingsley. (HSOP.)

Under Kingsley, Laurel Grove was enlarged and prospered. His African-born wife, Anna Madgigine Jai, purchased by Kingsley in 1806, was vital to his success. When freed in 1811, she skillfully ran the plantation in Zephaniah's absence. In 1813, everything changed. A group of Americans came into East Florida (as it had been named by the British) attempting to wrest it from Spanish control in an episode called the Patriots Rebellion. (SAF.)

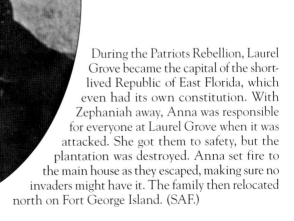

During the Patriots Rebellion, Laurel Grove became the capital of the short-lived Republic of East Florida, which even had its own constitution. With Zephaniah away, Anna was responsible for everyone at Laurel Grove when it was attacked. She got them to safety, but the plantation was destroyed. Anna set fire to the main house as they escaped, making sure no invaders might have it. The family then relocated north on Fort George Island. (SAF.)

In 1817, Zephaniah Kingsley purchased Fort George Island from John Houston McIntosh, a one-time leader of the failed Patriots Rebellion. McIntosh, in turn, purchased Laurel Grove and rebuilt it successfully. Operations included a sugar mill and a steam-powered sawmill, and McIntosh was considered the largest slave-owner in Clay County. In 1852, the $48,000 estate was purchased by Stephen Bryan. The plantation church (seen here) is its only structure ever to be photographed. (SAF.)

During the Civil War, the plantation suffered greatly. Stephen Bryan sold to Catherine Hookey, from Augusta, Georgia, who could not keep it going. She paid him $40,000 in Confederate money. After the war, Harriet Beecher Stowe (right) came to establish a farm with hopes of helping her son, Frederick, start his life again after being injured in battle. Her stay here was not long here. (Library of Congress, Prints & Photographs Division, item 2016652289.)

In 1876, Boston developer Washington Gano Benedict of the Florida Winter Home and Improvement Corporation bought Laurel Grove's 9,000 acres for $32,000. During the Reconstruction period, many northerners took advantage of low land prices and moved into the agricultural south. The condition of the former plantation was not impressive. Benedict had a lot of work to do. (SAF.)

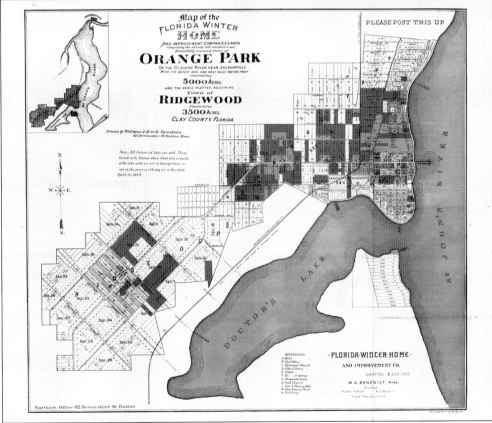

Benedict divided the land into farm and home lots. He donated land for a cemetery and churches and then planted orange trees on every home lot to entice northerners with the potential for ready-made income. Orange Park was born, officially recognized by the Florida Legislature in 1879. Benedict advertised it as "the healthiest state in the union" with "the best land in Florida for growing oranges." (TOP.)

Promotional efforts worked. People eagerly bought the lots, some as absentee owners who simply wanted the orange grove revenue but others looking for healthier environs. E.D. Sabin's General Store (seen here in 1881) had two stores a few yards from each other on Kingsley Avenue. The post office was in the store. A.L. Evans joined Sabin in 1882 and went on to be mayor and town treasurer. (SAF.)

Washington Gano Benedict provided land for churches when he designed the town. Grace Episcopal, shown here, established in 1880, is one of the town's oldest. On February 28, 1878, the Right Reverend John Freeman Young, bishop of the Diocese of Florida, convinced a friend, architect Robert Shuler, to design the church in its Gothic Revival style. The church still stands on Kingsley Avenue, and its old bell still rings. (SAF.)

Washington Gano Benedict also donated land for a Catholic church. The wooden structure in the 1880 photograph at right was at the corner of Reed and Stowe Streets. Named for Saint Catherine, the 54-seat structure served for many years before being moved, sold, and repurchased. In 1930, additions included gas lighting, a wood stove, and a portable organ. The original steeple's cross is kept inside the current St. Catherine's on Kingsley Avenue. (CCA.)

The seven-acre deed for Magnolia Cemetery was given to Orange Park in 1877 by Washington Benedict and his partner, Alpheus Blake of Boston. The oldest plots are on the main street, and many of the founding families can be found among the names. The gates are made from bricks that are over 100 years old from the old St. Luke's Hospital in Jacksonville. (HSOP.)

An African American community started to develop in Orange Park soon after incorporation. Working families settled north of Kingsley Avenue between Plainfield Avenue and US Highway 17: farmers who worked in fields and laborers who worked for turpentine companies or for the railroad. Orange Park's Turpentine Camp was located a short walk from where this community developed, in the area now known as Grove Park. (CCA.)

Washington Gano Benedict planted acres of oranges. A five-acre plot sold for $600 and included cleared, fenced land planted with 250 orange trees. Some northern buyers did not ever build on their lots but kept the land as an investment, reaping profits from the sale of oranges. This lasted until the great freezes of the 1890s, which froze the trees down to their roots, never to regrow. (HSOP.)

Two

PINES AND PIONEERS

Orange Park's climate had great recuperative qualities. Benjamin Stiles, seated on his porch at right, visited northeast Florida for health reasons every winter from 1868 to 1872. That year, his serious case of pneumonia was cured, and he decided to live in Orange Park year-round. He bought 60 acres on which he grew 2,300 orange trees, the largest grove in the area. He served as justice of the peace and mayor. (SAF.)

William Helffrich, a brilliant retired minister, was among the town's first residents. The 1880s brought a yellow fever epidemic sweeping the state. The newly constructed Helffrich house served as a makeshift hospital for the afflicted with the youngest Helffrich son, John, the physician in charge. He did not lose any patients, but his mother, Amanda Helffrich, suffered a severe infection, which convinced the family to move back to Pennsylvania. (CCA.)

The William Maierfeldt family, shown here in 1878 at its home on the corner of Milwaukee Avenue and present-day Park Avenue, was also among the founding families. William emigrated from northern Germany in 1869 with his wife and two-year-old son, Frederick. The family had settled in Milwaukee, Wisconsin, before being lured to Orange Park by Benedict's advertising. (CCA.)

The 1880s were interesting times for William Maierfeldt. A killer freeze came to threaten his strawberries years before the big freezes killed his oranges. The whole family worked for hours covering strawberry plants with pine straw and Spanish moss they had stockpiled for just this purpose. His forethought saved his berries when many other farmers were not so lucky. (CCA.)

Benedict encouraged the locals to join activities at his riverfront Park View House as evidence to visitors of the town's appeal. There were many dances held there. When grown, Frederick Maierfeldt (seen here near the hotel pavilion) met Christine Brandenburger, the daughter of Prussian immigrant farmers from Illinois. They were married and had sons William Carl and Frederick Kenneth and daughter Nancy Christine. (CCA.)

The Maierfeldt family operated a successful truck farm for 40 years and an orange grove that included 600 trees. They had 17 acres of fine peach trees, strawberries, tomatoes, and Irish potatoes. Before a good road could be put in, all transport, produce and human, was by steamboat. There are a good number of Maierfeldt photographs, suggesting economic comfort and productivity on their farm. (CCA.)

William Maierfeldt told stories of steamboats and shenanigans, of enterprise and experiments that entertained generations of his family. The children in the rubber suits seen here lived simple, charmed lives. William's stories were written into a small book, *Early Days in Orange Park*, by his grandson, also named William Maierfeldt, years later. Copies are still available. (CCA.)

Transportation and communication were mostly done via the river in the early days of the town. The *May Garner*, seen here, was a vital link following a regular, reliable route. It picked passengers up in Orange Park from the Kingsley pier, then went to Green Cove Springs, then Jacksonville and on to Mandarin in daily runs morning and evening. William Maierfeldt's little book of memories reveals much about this travel. (CCA.)

St. James Chapel, an African Methodist Episcopal church, was established in 1879 at the intersection of Mound and McIntosh Streets. In 1880, Washington Gano Benedict conveyed the property to the trustees of the church. The deed states that a building was on the property at the time. The present structure was constructed in the same location in 1914. (University of North Florida [UNF], Thomas G. Carpenter Library, Special Collections and University Archives, George Lansing Taylor Jr. Collection.)

An expanding African American population led to another church near St. James AME. In 1881, R.W. Wheeler and A. Anderson helped organize St. John Missionary Baptist Church on Mound Street. By 1900, the community included a grocer, general store keeper, carpenter, preacher, sawmill laborers, railroad section hands and porters, and domestic servants. By 1917, the neighborhood consisted of approximately 15 buildings, including a church, school, and residences. (UNF, Thomas G. Carpenter Library, Special Collections and University Archives, George Lansing Taylor Jr. Collection.)

On March 6, 1884, the Jacksonville, Tampa & Key West Railroad came to Orange Park. It offered morning and afternoon departures to Palatka and brought a new shipping alternative to local farmers. The trip took only two and one-half hours. William Maierfeldt reported proudly that all the line's original rails, from Jacksonville to Tampa, had to be changed to standard gauge, and it was done in just one day. (CCA.)

LEONIDAS ELIJAH WADE, Jacksonville, Florida.

"HAPPY"

LL. B. Course ; John Marshall Debating Society.

Pause, kind reader, and for a second let your eyes wander upward to the smile that adorns this page. There now, once more; good. This is Happy—but not he of the Sunday Times. This is Wade—but not within the inscription on Belshazzar's palace hall. No; this is plain Leonidas Happy Wade, or Happy Leonidas Wade, at your service. Here is a man who will go out of his way to do you a kindness. As a law student he makes good, and he has that degree of perseverance that means a making. You cannot discourage him. His friends agree that Happy, indeed should be, he who is happy.

Leonidas Wade had to start working at an early age when his father died in 1868, leaving a family of seven behind. He made 25¢ per day for his labors and studied by himself at night by firelight. He taught school, worked on farms, split rails, and built dams to earn the money he needed to make his way in the world. This image is from the 1905 University of Florida yearbook. (HSOP.)

Wade moved to Florida in 1879, working in orange groves, on steamboats, and in a hardware store in Jacksonville. He continued his studies and bought the area then known as Seminole Springs. After renaming the area Wadesboro Springs, he bottled and sold the water during the late 1880s. The famous Flagler hotels in St. Augustine were his prime customers. (CCA.)

Wade became a criminal defense attorney and member of the Florida House of Representatives. In 1918, he came out in support of women's suffrage. His name is readily found in records of old criminal cases in Florida law books. The life of Leonidas Wade is a perfect example of the American Dream. He used his clear mind, sound body, and heroic determination to triumph over obstacles. (CCA.)

During the early days of the Florida Winter Home and Improvement Company's recruitment of tourists and settlers, the springs assumed a variety of names: Tallulah Springs (with varied spellings), Springfield, Old Mill Springs, Roaring Magnetic (or Magnetic Roaring) Springs, Bryant Springs, Maple Springs, Seminole Springs, Wadesboro Springs, Camp Echokotee Springs, and finally, W.W. Gay Spring. (HSOP.)

The promotional pamphlet *Florida, the Healthiest State in the Union: Orange Park, near Jacksonville, One of Its Greatest Attractions* describes the spring as "a fine medicinal roaring spring, slightly impregnated with white sulphur, [that] . . . with a discharge of 2,000 gallons per minute, with a temperature of 72 degrees, and having a fall of 15 feet to the lake, is of great value to the property." (HSOP.)

Steamboats brought nearby residents from Mandarin and Jacksonville to Orange Park to enjoy the refreshing mineral waters of these springs. Postcards, stereographs, and glowing advertisement descriptions led to excursions "five miles into the pine woods" from Hotel Marion to the springs on a regular schedule for the medicinal benefits to be obtained from drinking and bathing in the water. (HSOP.)

27

The Horton family, seen here, has a long and colorful history with the town. Henry Hezekiah Horton built Horton Lumber and Saw Mill on Doctors Lake in 1883. It turned out 7,500 feet of lumber per day and employed seven men. It used a 25-horsepower engine to make boards, laths, and shingles. The composition of Doctors Lake is such that sawdust from Horton's mill can still be brought up today. (CCA.)

Tan and Annie McDower (seen here) came to live on Orange Park's Railroad Avenue in the 1920s, having courageously escaped from an oppressive turpentine company in Florida's Big Bend area. Tan used his mechanical ability and turpentine experience well. All through the Great Depression, the McDowers did okay because Tan could instinctively forecast to the barrel how much each group of trees would produce in its lifetime. (CCA.)

This 1893 home was constructed by and for Joseph Green, a prominent African American carpenter from Mississippi. Located on McIntosh Avenue, it was near the St. James AME Church. Greene built 15 homes in town, but this one's unique ethnic heritage earned it a spot in the National Register of Historic Places. (National Register of Historic Places.)

After Joseph Green's death in June 1928, his wife, Annie, remained in this home until her death in 1953. It was sold by Green's daughter-in-law in 1994 to St. James AME Church to be used as a rental property. The house was demolished in 1999 after a heated battle by Betty Demmons, who had helped get it in the National Register. Its legacy now lies only in old images. (National Register of Historic Places.)

In the early days of Orange Park, it was still legal to force convicts (who often lived in state-run camps) to do the difficult and dangerous labor to make turpentine. That practice was stopped in 1923, and there is no record of it having been used in Orange Park. Instead, those men who worked the trees in Orange Park relocated to the town by choice to find such employment. (Mary Jo McTammany.)

Mary Fillmore grew up in the area developed by Joseph Green near the railroad tracks. She became a business leader in the black community. She owned a tavern and restaurant on Kingsley Avenue and managed family rental properties. Her brothers, Solomon (also known as "Bub"), George, Dave, and Sonny, were successful commercial fishermen. Some of the land they owned is still in the hands of family descendants. (SAF.)

The William Ball House was built in 1878. It was described by the National Register of Historic Places as a "unique structure, painted in different shades of green." Ball had come down from Plainfield, New Jersey, as one of the first families to live on the new street named, aptly enough, Plainfield Avenue. He came to be a citrus farmer, lured by Washington Gano Benedict's endorsements of the area. (HSOP.)

In 1905, Harry Horton Jr. built a general store with living quarters on the second floor facing Smith Street. He acted as postman in 1906 and 1907. The 1913 Horton family house is pictured above. In 1928, Horton also built a concrete block house on Kingsley Avenue with handmade blocks and reportedly reinforced the foundation with railroad ties. (CCA.)

Harry Horton Jr., like his father, was involved in several businesses. He devised a refrigeration system for steamboats to keep berries fresh. At the foot of Kingsley Avenue sat the town's 1,400-foot pier, where Horton also operated a pavilion to sell cool refreshments to tourists. Harry Horton Jr.'s Stanley Steamer, pictured here, was registered with the state in 1913, the first of its kind in the town. (HSOP.)

Kingsley Avenue was a two-lane road with a park in the middle, each lane flanked by a triple row of live and water oaks. Look closely to see the free-ranging pig on the street. The livestock that wandered around town carried with it some unwanted health concerns and became the subject of a campaign, championed by women of the town, that eventually mandated fencing. (HSOP.)

William E. Parmenter Jr., shown here in his Plainfield Avenue home, lived in Orange Park from 1883 until 1932. He graduated from Harvard in 1877 with an artium baccalaureus degree. He left Boston for farm life and was especially proud of his Berkshire pigs. On June 6, 1894, he married Ione F. Fisher. Two of their three children survived to adulthood: Mary Helen and William George Parmenter. (SAF.)

The Parmenter home was built as a kitchen with a bedroom above it, creating a two-story structure. After he married, he added five rooms and a front porch. This walkway led to the family's swimming pool. The Parmenters starred in or directed shows at Orange Park's Laurel Pleasure Club theater, and neighbors often borrowed books from their expansive library. (SAF.)

Like his neighbors, Parmenter grew vegetables and strawberries and took an active role in the development and politics of the community. He served several times on the town council and as mayor of Orange Park. This 1896 picture, taken with his wife and daughter, Mary, shows most of their two-acre lot on Plainfield Avenue. (SAF.)

Joseph Tarr Copeland had a long political history in Michigan before coming to Orange Park in 1878. He was a Union general and a justice of the peace in Maine and Florida. He was postmaster of New Portland, Maine, then of Lake Orchid, Michigan, and finally of Orange Park. He was also Clay County judge before he died in Orange Park on his 80th birthday, May 6, 1893. (Greater West Bloomfield Historical Society.)

Three

TOURISM

Washington Gano Benedict began work on a hotel for Orange Park almost immediately after the purchase of old Laurel Grove's land was finalized. He built the Park View House near an already established dock at the foot of Kingsley Avenue, which he expanded to accommodate steamboats bringing northern tourists and prospective settlers. (HSOP.)

To attract the attention of steamboats on the St. Johns River, Benedict placed a 200-foot-long sign near the hotel. The sign faced the river and could be read easily by traveling tourists. If there were not enough guests in the hotel, Benedict would ride his horse through town, inviting locals to come to dances and, thereby, make the town seem more cosmopolitan to paying guests. (SAF.)

That first Park View House burned in 1881 but was quickly rebuilt. The new Park View Hotel was a frame building with wide porches that contained 40 rooms. A 14-room house stood in the rear of the hotel to accommodate additional guests as needed. An English immigrant named Edmund Holt subsequently purchased the hotel and settled in the town. (HSOP.)

In 1879, a big celebration of the nation's 103rd birthday took place on the hotel grounds, carefully planned and advertised for a very large crowd. There were athletic contests and boat races, all offering cash prizes, some up to $1. All competitors paid a 25¢ entrance fee for a chance to win prizes and local fame. The evening was capped off with a fireworks display on the St. Johns River. (HSOP.)

Many wealthy visitors stayed at the Park View, some after docking their yachts there. William Astor, whose name was given to a street in Orange Park, often stayed at the Park View. Among other things, Astor contributed financially to the construction of the Grace Episcopal Chapel, which was completed in 1878. (HSOP.)

The 1880s-era archaeologist Clarence B. Moore identified two Native burial mounds in Orange Park. These were largely made of sand, and by the time tourists began visiting, they had already been greatly altered. Washington Gano Benedict encouraged visitors, like the Philadelphia man above, to pose for photographs with the mounds and perhaps try their luck at finding artifacts there. (Mary Jo McTammany.)

Among the most famous guests at the first hotel were Pres. Ulysses S. Grant and Philip H. Sheridan. They visited Orange Park as part of their grand tour of Florida in 1880, along with their wives. Business was good, as many northerners came during winter, often for the health benefits of fresh air and sunshine for family members recovering from tuberculosis and other conditions. (SAF.)

Arriving on the same steamboat as Grant was Burdette J. Johnson, founder of the Johnson Soap Company. He boarded at the Park View while seeking help for his daughter, Karrie, suffering from consumption. Karrie's recovery led to a lasting bond between Johnson's family and Orange Park. By 1885, Johnson was a director of the Florida Winter Home and Improvement Company. (HSOP.)

Newspapers, almanacs, and postcards printed in the late 1800s multiplied across the nation. With industrialized printing machines and the telegraph, newspapers shared one another's stories wirelessly. They filled their large pages of print with words but few pictures. Colorized postcards were penned by tourists extolling the beauty of places in vivid prose and, often, poetry as well. (HSOP.)

Steamboats were vital to Florida. The *May Garner* was one of several steamboats that carried passengers to and from Orange Park. It was 93 feet long and 17 feet, 6 inches across the waterline. The deck was roomy enough for 150 passengers. It was launched in 1893 and served until the 1920s, when it was accidentally burned. William Maierfeldt wrote, "You should not be surprised when getting aboard, to see a 12-foot-alligator tied down on a 12-foot-board" lashed to the deck.

Oskey's, a store that catered to tourists wanting souvenirs of Florida, bought gators to transform them into handbags, shoes, belts, or suitcases. Also on deck were wicker baskets of bread from the Rosenbush Bakery in Green Cove Springs, crates of live chickens, tied-up pigs, and even hobbled horses or cattle. These were commonplace to *May Garner* passengers. (CCA.)

There are widely repeated reports that Buffalo Bill Cody and Chief Sitting Bull visited Orange Park in 1880. However, there are many unanswered questions about this claim. The traveling Wild West Show had not yet been developed, and yet the names above are signed into the hotel register for July 1880. There are no photographs of this event known to exist and no newspaper reports. The event is tantalizingly mysterious. (Library of Congress.)

D. F. BARRY,
WEST SUPERIOR,
WIS.

SITTING BULL AND BUFFALO BILL.
Copyrighted 1897.

The hotel changed throughout the years. It ultimately claimed 65 rooms, a golf course, sulfur water baths, and welcoming gingerbread-trimmed verandas that wrapped two floors. Society pages in newspapers around the country boasted of visitors and their activities in Orange Park's fine hotel. By 1890, Edmund Holt enlarged the hotel and renamed it Hotel Marion, in honor of his wife. This is the familiar name for the hotel. (CCA.)

For a few years in the early 1910s, the hotel was called the Sparhawk, but that name did not stick. The name "Hotel Marion" returned and has remained the most identified with the structure. Advertisements were posted in all large northern cities, and business stayed good as the town's population passed 700. (HSOP.)

The years following World War I saw further growth in the town. The steamboats began to be less popular as railroads came to Florida. The hotel still did good business with its regular visitors, especially during wintertime. Local citizens provided labor to the hotel to supplement farm income and break up some of the monotony. (HSOP.)

The old hotel was showing its age by 1922, when the Loyal Order of the Moose purchased the hotel and surrounding acreage from then-owner Charles A. Brown Jr. for approximately $50,000. The first residents came from Moosehart, Indiana (national home of the Loyal Order of the Moose), with a two-year trial lease for what was then considered to be a winter resort property. (Mary Jo McTammany.)

THE MARTIN, ORANGE PARK, FLORIDA.

"City of Contentment" was established on 26 acres. Moose supreme secretary Rodney H. Brandon purchased the property on the banks of the St. Johns River. The original concept was to "organize the residents so that they might help each other and help themselves, and provide from their own energy the major part of the cost of their keep." (HSOP.)

Florida was changing. It became the first state to legalize betting on greyhound racing in 1931. It was also the last state to ban it. Orange Park's first attempt was in 1926, when Sam Schwietzer formed the Seminole Kennel Club along with W.R. Carter and James V. Wilson. They sold individual shares of the club, making it seem private, but invited thousands of "guests" to their event. County police shut them down. (CCA.)

The Clay County Kennel Club was opened in 1931 on the same site as the Seminole. Lasting for five years, it presented the problems such a venture involved and struggled to find solutions for those. Various local jobs were created, including those for women in the concession stand and off-duty police constable A.H. Harrington, who was there to keep the peace inside the club. (HSOP.)

From 1935 through 1945, there was no racing in town. In January 1946, Orange Park Kennel Club was opened, and it has been a presence ever since. By 1947, there were 190 telephones on the town's local exchange and lots of traffic going through town. That was good for the kennel club, which was part of a seasonal racing circuit with Bayard Raceways and Jacksonville Kennel Club for many years. (SAF.)

After World War II ended, a group of investors created the Florida Driving Club on a large tract of undeveloped Wells Road. With Paul Reinhold as president, the club was elegantly presented to draw harness racing and horse show aficionados. Launched with a gala two-day opening in October 1946, it ultimately did not last. Failing to get gambling certification meant no betting, so the organizers wound up boarding horses instead. (SAF.)

The old hotel, renamed Brandon Hall, was covered with cobblestones. It remained in use until its demolition in 1951. According to the May 1968 *Moose* magazine, "It was largely through the inspiration and urging of Mr. Brandon, as Grand Regent of the Legation of the Moose, with the aid of the Women of the Moose, that Moosehaven, the 'City of Contentment' . . . at Orange Park, Florida, was financed and established." (CCA.)

Cars eventually took the place of steamboats for tourist transportation. During the mid-1920s, US Highway 17 was extended through Orange Park. The large hotel era faded away only to be replaced in the 1950s and 1960s by motels and motor inns. Several different such accommodations dotted Park Avenue from that time forwards. This was reinforced by the addition of Highway 295 and the Buckman Bridge by 1970. (HSOP.)

Amidst much controversy, the BestBet Poker Room was added to the kennel club in 2008. With a 3-2 vote, the town council accepted additional gambling. Mayor Bob Standifer, very opposed, did not want the town to profit from people's losses, and Councilman Ron Raymond stormed out, yelling, "Sell out!" Greyhound racing will end in December 2020, due to legislation passed by the state legislature, but the poker room continues. (HSOP.)

By 2014, while Tasha Hyder coordinated events for the town, farmers' markets, Reel Fun Nights, and KidsFest were introduced. KidsFest was a huge success, with over 10,000 people attending, and has become an annual event. This fun, educational event has won regional SUNsational Awards at the Florida Festival & Events Association Annual Conference. Farmers' markets are also open on dedicated Sundays. (TOP.)

Four

MAKING A LIVING IN EARLY ORANGE PARK

Washington Gano Benedict understood that for the town to be a success, there must be other employment opportunities besides farming. As he successfully developed tourist interest, he simultaneously developed industry. He encouraged the development of industries that took advantage of the area's natural resources. From the town's bounty came large-scale businesses, primarily farms, fish, and factories. (CCA.)

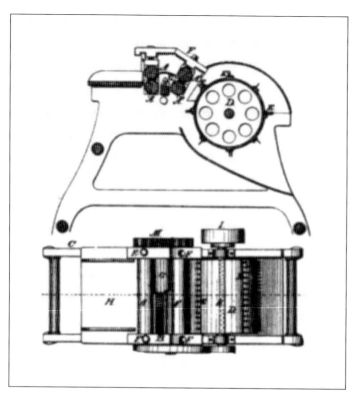

What some saw as a nuisance, Benedict saw as an asset. On December 27, 1877, Patent 201,269 (diagram at right) was filed for "Machines for Treating Palmetto Leaves, Etc." by George F. Miller and Washington Gano Benedict. It specified "a new and useful Improvement in Machinery for Cutting, Stripping or Combing into Shreds all Varieties of Palmetto Leaves, Stalks, or Buds to be used in manufacture and all upholstery purposes." (HSOP.)

The wooden palmetto factory building was located on McIntosh Street, near today's Moosehaven entrance. It employed women into the 1880s, making hats, bags, fans, and more from palmetto leaves. Women were ideal employees because the work was delicate and repetitive and did not require masculine strength. This allowed employers to pay less for their salaries but gave the women a respectable way to earn money. (Library of Congress.)

On March 30, 1878, another patent (203,177) was filed for "Treating Palmetto Fiber for Use in the Arts" by George F. Miller and Washington Gano Benedict. This one applied the fibers to the production of rope, "twisting the fibers while wet, then drying, and afterward picking apart for use." This provided for less-utile, more-decorative applications of the fiber. (SAF.)

3. The combination, with the sections b' b' and spring-catch e, of the projections f, substantially as described.

ARNOLD MESSLER.

Witnesses:
JOSEPH A. MILLER,
IRA A. SEAMANS.

201,269. MACHINES FOR TREATING PALMETTO-LEAVES, &c. George F. Miller, Jacksonville, and W. G. Benedict, Orange Park, Fla.; said Miller assignor to said Benedict. Filed Dec. 27, 1877.

To all whom it may concern:

Be it known that we, GEORGE F. MILLER, of the city of Jacksonville, in the county of Duval and State of Florida, and WASHINGTON G. BENEDICT, of the villa of Orange Park, in the county of Clay and State of Florida, have jointly invented a new and useful Improvement in Machines for Cutting, Stripping, or Combing into Shreds all Varieties of Palmetto Leaves, Stalks, or Buds, to be used for and in the manufacture of bedding and all upholstery purposes, of which the following is a specification:

Figure 1 is a sectional view, and Fig. 2 is a top view.

The object of our invention is to make a machine which will strip palmetto leaves, stalks, and buds into fine fibers, so that it can be braided or twisted, and make an article of commerce similar to the curled hair used by upholsterers.

The particular features of novelty in our invention will be pointed out hereinafter, and specifically claimed.

A suitable frame, C, supports the operative parts of our machine, having at one end a feed-board, H, on which the leaves, &c., to be stripped are placed. The leaves, &c., are fed from this board to the feed-rollers A A, which draw them forward against a series of knives, B, which knives split the leaves, &c., into strips. These knives B are preferably placed about three-eighths of an inch apart; but a greater or less width may be given them.

The leaves, &c., are of such strength or stiffness that the feed-rollers A A will push them against the knives B, and, after the splitting, will carry the points forward to the feed-rollers A′ A′. A shield or guide, G, is placed above the knives to prevent the ends of the leaves rising up, and may be curved, as shown, to deflect them downward, where the construction of the machine requires it.

The feed-rollers A A and A′ A′ are held a suitable distance apart by set-screws F F, and may, if desired, have a spring-pressure upon the leaves, &c., passing through them.

After the ends of the split leaves, &c., have passed through the rollers A A and A′ A′ they are caught by the stripping pins or combs E on the wheel or drum D. This drum

D revolves with greater velocity than the feed-rollers, and the teeth have the effect of combing or stripping the leaves, &c., into fine fibers. The shield or apron over the combing-drum holds down the leaves, &c., so they can be acted upon by the teeth.

The teeth E on the drum D do not project directly from the cylindrical surface of the drum, but are placed in rows on slats or ridges running lengthwise of the cylinder. This is to prevent the fiber from clinging to and winding upon the drum, which it will do if the teeth simply project from the surface of the drum.

The points of the palmetto-leaves, &c., are tied together, and the leaves fed point first to the first set of feed-rollers.

The speed of the feed-rollers is regulated by gearing, so that the leaves, &c., can be moved with more or less rapidity as compared with that of the combing-drum D.

The teeth of the combing-drum D may be made adjustable as to their distance from each other, so as to vary the width of the shreds of the leaf, to adapt it to the varying requirements of the manufactures in which it is used.

We claim as new—

1. The combination of the feed-rolls A A and A′ A′ and intermediate slitting-knives B, adapted to make a continuous cut, constructed substantially as described.

2. The combination of the slitting-knives B, the rollers A A, and the guide or shield G, to hold the leaves, &c., or other material, down to the knives.

3. The combination of the feed-rolls A A and A′ A′, the slitting-knives located between them, and the shield or guide G, substantially as described.

4. The combination of the slitting-knives and the combing-drum, substantially as described.

5. The combination of the feed-board, two sets of feed-rolls, with slitting-knives between them, the shield or guide over these knives, and the combing-drum, when all are constructed, arranged, and operated substantially as described.

GEORGE F. MILLER.
WASHINGTON G. BENEDICT.

Witnesses:
M. C. JORDAN,
C. H. FLOWERS.

201,270. GAS-REGULATORS. John Miller, Jr., Philadelphia, Pa. Filed Nov. 13, 1877.

To all whom it may concern:

Be it known that I, JOHN MILLER, Jr., of Philadelphia, in the county of Philadelphia and State of Pennsylvania, have invented certain new and useful Improvements in Gas-Regulators; and I do hereby declare the following to be a full, clear, and exact description of the invention, such as will enable

Northern editorials from 1879 touted Orange Park's suitability for dairies and chicken farming. With glowing endorsements of abundant land and convenient steamboat shipping, they claimed Florida's cattlemen needed only to provide a few ears of corn per day. Further, Orange Park's "genial climate for growing fowl" lured prospective chicken farmers from as far away as Vermont with the promise of a ready-made, growing market. (HSOP.)

Another place of employment in early Orange Park was the Moss Factory. A group of wooden sheds stood just east of the railroad tracks with a production line system of tasks. Locals, including children, were paid to collect Spanish moss and deliver it to the factory. To collect the moss, locals used bamboo poles with wire wrapped around their ends to pull the fibers from the trees. (HSOP.)

When taken to the factory, the moss would be boiled over an open fire to remove bugs and sap. Once boiled, the moss was laid out to dry and then packed in bales to be sent to northern factories for use in furniture cushions and bedding. Conveniently located near the railroad, the process from trees to trains was expedient. (HSOP.)

Harry Horton's businesses kept him hopping. Several lawsuits were filed by and against him. In 1903, Horton sued a Mr. Morrison for killing his hogs with a shotgun. (There was no judgment in the files for the killed hogs.) In 1907, the Jacksonville Grocery Company sued Horton for nonpayment. He was in litigation so often no one was surprised if did not even appear on court dates. (CCA.)

Jesse Carnes was a businessman and Orange Park's mayor in 1919 and again in 1933. He owned Carnes Fish House, which started in 1893 at the end of Kingsley Avenue but moved to Doctors Lake in 1914. It packed and shipped fish all along the East Coast. The Carnes Fish House paid 3–5¢ per pound for unskinned catfish and 6–9¢ for dressed cats. (CCA.)

The farmers' co-op building above, labeled "Clay County Grocery Co. Wholesale," was built and maintained by area farmers to provide space for packing and shipping crops, conveniently adjacent to the train station. To transport strawberries and other produce efficiently, they used the same refrigeration system built by Harry Horton for steamboats. (CCA.)

Once cars became a family necessity, Orange Park's business opportunities blossomed. Traffic between Jacksonville and Green Cove Springs became a steady stream that continues still in the town. Car dealerships, repair shops, and gas stations multiplied as America took to the streets. As land became more pricey, businesses shared parking lots, creating early versions of strip malls, which provided welcome employment for locals. (HSOP.)

James and Pauline Wylie, seen here, came to Florida in 1912. Previously working as trapeze artists with the Campbell Bros. Circus, he played banjo, and she sang and danced. James served on the town council in the late 1930s and was mayor of Orange Park twice. Wylie's Store was the center of life for the town. When electricity came in 1923, Wylie added an electric repair shop and soda fountain. (CCA.)

The Henry Howard family, seen here, ran this one-room store to supplement farm income in the 1920s. Built on Plainfield Avenue from pines cut down the street, it sold cold drinks, candy, and staples. When it was demolished, a Howard family home was built in its place. Howard family members seated in front of Henry Howard Sr. (straw hat, left) are, from left to right, Evelyn Alveniah, Alice May, Laurence Edgar, Franklin Eldridge, Henry Jr., and Alice Inez. (CCA.)

Self-employed African American businessman Lawrence Hicks was Orange Park's "Ice Man" in the 1940s. This small structure stored ice to be sold and delivered to customers' iceboxes. Some locals remember buying it to make ice cream in Florida's hot summers. A few recall boys sneaking into the icehouse to cool off and the kindness of Hicks, grinning and saying, "Just close the door when you leave." (HSOP.)

As the city of Jacksonville grew, so did traffic through Orange Park. In the early 1940s, this led the way to establishing several motor inns and motels along the new Highway 17, which replaced several smaller roads into Jacksonville. The Azalea Court cabins, seen here, invited visitors to "rest among the pines" in "steam-heated cabins" with "private baths." (HSOP.)

Louis and William Huntley, Clay County natives, were prosperous businessmen starting in the 1940s. The brothers were active in community affairs and developed several businesses, including a convenience store chain with over 340 locations at one time. The brothers were active in community government and corporate affairs for the region for decades. (CCA.)

In 1947, Stockton, Whatley, Davin of Jacksonville developed a new community in Orange Park, calling it Holly Point. It was located at the juncture of the St. Johns River and Doctors Lake, offering waterfront and wooded lots ranging from $900 to $3,500 per lot. Large full-page ads were taken out to promote the development, touting "cool summer living and rigid building restrictions to insure high standards for architecture and construction." (Brad Officer Realtor Group.)

Dr. Marcus B. Bergh established the first hospital in Orange Park. As medical director of Moosehaven, he was often called upon when locals needed medical care. Seeing the need for a medical facility for the town, he established the Pureal Medical Center in the early 1950s. For over 40 years, he served the medical, surgical, and obstetrical needs of Orange Park and became much-beloved by his patients. (HSOP.)

In 2005, after 31 years as an Orange Park institution, the Sisters Tea Room closed. The restaurant featured lattice and lace and waitresses wearing long, prairie-style dresses. Sisters Gwen Chojnacki and Bobbie Jo Robbins went from housewives to entrepreneurs, providing a unique atmosphere for generations. Specialties lovingly remembered included hummingbird cake, chicken salad, and pies. Many showers, birthdays, and other events were hosted by the sisters. (HSOP.)

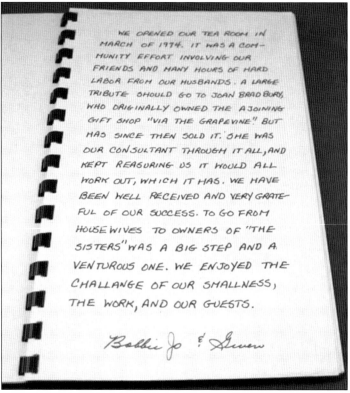

WE OPENED OUR TEA ROOM IN MARCH OF 1974. IT WAS A COMMUNITY EFFORT INVOLVING OUR FRIENDS AND MANY HOURS OF HARD LABOR FROM OUR HUSBANDS. A LARGE TRIBUTE SHOULD GO TO JOAN BRADBURY, WHO ORIGINALLY OWNED THE ADJOINING GIFT SHOP "VIA THE GRAPEVINE" BUT HAS SINCE THEN SOLD IT. SHE WAS OUR CONSULTANT THROUGH IT ALL, AND KEPT REASURING US IT WOULD ALL WORK OUT, WHICH IT HAS. WE HAVE BEEN WELL RECEIVED AND VERY GRATEFUL OF OUR SUCCESS. TO GO FROM HOUSEWIVES TO OWNERS OF "THE SISTERS" WAS A BIG STEP AND A VENTUROUS ONE. WE ENJOYED THE CHALLANGE OF OUR SMALLNESS, THE WORK, AND OUR GUESTS.

Bobbie Jo & Gwen

Five

ORANGE PARK NORMAL AND INDUSTRIAL SCHOOL

As Orange Park was becoming a town, America's Reconstruction period ended, and Florida came under Democratic leadership again. Civil rights for blacks diminished, segregation was legalized, and funding for education for blacks was reduced, making black schools more rigorous. In 1888, Daniel Hand, a northern philanthropist, stepped forward, giving a $1-million endowment to the American Missionary Association (AMA) for the purpose of providing blacks with vocational training. (CCA.)

The AMA visited Orange Park and found a good parcel of land with many northern transplant residents and a great need for an African American school. It accepted the land and began construction in early 1891. Thus the Orange Park Normal and Industrial School opened on October 7, 1891, with 26 students. Amos N. Farnham, the first principal, directed an excellent faculty of northern teachers focused on preparing black teachers. (CCA.)

The campus stretched over an entire block facing Kingsley Avenue. The town donated the land with the understanding that children from the town would be able to attend, whether black or white. Just two months after the opening of the school, Daniel Hand passed away. The school would thereafter be called "the Hand School" by many. (CCA.)

GIRLS WASHING UNDER THE PINES

At the start, the campus consisted of 10 acres of oak and orange trees, several classrooms, two dormitories, and a two-story industrial building. By the fall of 1892, there were 116 students, some from out of state, as well as some in the higher grades, proving the school was attracting intelligent and appreciative patrons. In addition to regular classes, the school taught stenography, typing, agriculture, horticulture, and printing. (CCA.)

Orange Park Normal and Industrial School was the only school for miles around that was conducted with any regularity and efficiency. A few local whites began to send their children to the school. As white confidence increased, so did white enrollment. By 1894, there were 35 white students. Ironically, the school did so well that it drew attention to itself. (CCA.)

In 1893, William N. Sheats became superintendent of public instruction. He personified the white supremacy that insisted on strict segregation and no political rights for blacks. A foe of interracial education, he refused to employ anyone educated in mixed schools and made teacher certification requirements more demanding. The new rules led to a greater shortage of black teachers and fewer educational opportunities for black students. (CCA.)

State law, at the time, only prohibited integrated public schools. The state's newest constitution (1885) said, "White and colored children shall not be taught in the same school, but impartial provision shall be made for both." Orange Park Normal and Industrial School, however, was a private school. Director Farnum explained to Sheats that students at the school were kind to each other, generally self-segregating within any mixed spaces. (CCA.)

William Sheats began a lobbying campaign to force the Orange Park school to honor his views. He asked the legislature to extend the law to private schools as well. In May 1895, the legislature passed a law that carried a $500 fine or three-month prison sentence in the county jail if violated. The AMA, with support from northern journals, fought back in print to defy Sheats's law. (CCA.)

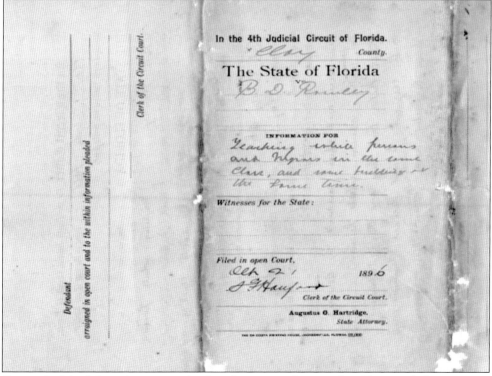

Orange Park had the only private school in the state at the time that Sheats railed against as a "nest of vile fanatics." He got the county law enforcement involved. Indictments were handed down on April 6, 1896. Four days later, Principal B.D. Rowlee, five teachers, three white patrons, and the local Congregational minister were arrested for violating Sheats's law. The school was closed for the remainder of the term. (CCA.)

The AMA hired Jacksonville attorneys Horatio Bisbee and Clement Rinehart. They argued successfully in court that the 14th Amendment was violated by the wording of the act's title. The school reopened and continued to operate for a few years, with few white students due to their parents being intimidated by Sheats's law. Bisbee had served four terms in the US House of Representatives before the normal school opened. (HSOP.)

In December 1917, the AMA closed the Orange Park school. That left only one normal school for blacks in the state, which was located in Tallahassee. The property was sold to the Children's Home Society in 1923 but went unused. It was sold to Moosehaven in 1927 and later was transferred to the Town of Orange Park. The carpentry shop was the last remaining building. (CCA.)

Six

The Monkey Farm

Psychobiologist Robert Yerkes first made a name for himself at Harvard University, during which time he developed an army intelligence test used during World War I. In 1924, he moved to Yale's new Institute of Human Comparative Psychology and became fascinated with the study of chimps and bonobos. He started with four animals in the Anthropoid Experiment Station of Yale but soon needed more space. (HSOP.)

Studying a gorilla on the estate of James Burbridge in Jacksonville in 1925 exposed Robert Yerkes to Florida's potential. The climate was ideal for apes. With wife Ada, he toured Florida before settling on secluded Orange Park, just south of Burbridge, as a potential laboratory site. It had a small railroad and minimal population, which ensured privacy. He found 187 acres just outside the town limits and commenced fundraising. (HSOP.)

With the financial support of Yale and Harvard Universities and philanthropic organizations such as Carnegie and Rockefeller, Robert Yerkes established the Yale Laboratories of Primate Biology, dubbed "the Monkey Farm" by locals. This watercolor of the physiology building was done in 1930 by David Yerkes, son of the founder. The original is archived at Yale. (Robert Mearns Yerkes Papers, Manuscripts and Archives, Yale University Library.)

Robert Yerkes's wife, Ada, a respected botanist in her own right, planned the landscaping for the laboratories. She also teamed up with Robert in field studies and publications. They coauthored important psychological research studies. Following Robert's death in 1956, she continued efforts on behalf of the station and worked to preserve its reputation. She, with her son David and daughter Roberta, saw to it that Robert's papers were archived. (Emory University Stuart A. Rose Manuscript, Archives & Rare Book Library.)

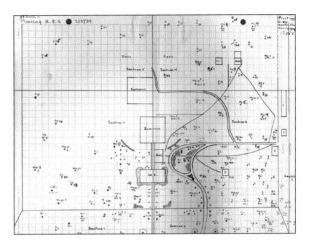

The laboratories started with nine buildings and 20 animals from Africa and Cuba. A seven-foot-high chain-link fence surrounded the station. Due to breeding activities, the colony grew to 40 animals. More facilities were needed. Developer Clyde Harris drew this rendering of a new physiology building in 1936 as part of a proposal to expand. The complex was almost double its original size by 1939. (Emory University Stuart A. Rose Manuscript, Archives & Rare Book Library.)

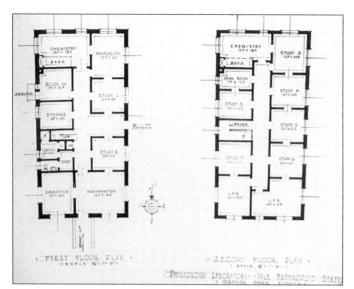

The station then included the new physiology building (shown here), a nursery (importing animals was no longer needed), a maternity building with four cages, and a small hospital building. The land increased to 200 acres. Scientists dealt with mosquitos, odd-tasting water, and free-ranging livestock. Some work continued at the New Haven labs, but all breeding was done in Orange Park. (Emory University Stuart A. Rose Manuscript, Archives & Rare Book Library.)

Field research done at the Monkey Farm ranged from animal cognition studies to drug addiction experiments. Anatomy, pathology, nutrition, and growth and development were examined. The most popularly chronicled studies reflected similarities with human beings. Social interaction, emotions, and status structures of chimps, gorillas, and bonobos parallel those in people. (CCA.)

When Dr. Yerkes retired in 1941, leadership was assumed by Dr. Karl Lashley, an eminent scientist who had been there for years, and Dr. Henry Nissen (pictured here), scientist and able administrator. Nissen, dedicated to his work, suffered a painful back injury when working with a mother ape who had just given birth. Her defensive instincts left Nissen in pain for the remainder of his life. (CCA.)

On July 1, 1942, the laboratory name was officially changed to honor its founder. It became the Yerkes Laboratories of Primate Biology, Inc. Management was reorganized, and Dr. Lashley was named as director. Lashley continued to focus on research, however, leaving most of the day-to-day management to Henry Nissen. (Emory University Stuart A. Rose Manuscript, Archives & Rare Book Library.)

The war years were hard for the lab's scientists. Housing was in great demand in Orange Park due to the nearby Naval Air Station Jacksonville. Scientists had to make way for servicemen and their families, many of whom remained in the town after the war ended. Marriages suffered, as the climate and conditions took a toll on relationships. Still, the work continued. (CCA.)

Keith and Cathy Hayes joined the staff of the laboratories in 1947. Keith worked on various projects, while Cathy focused on a long-term experiment to raise a chimpanzee as a human child. Viki, a three-day-old chimp, was adopted and taken to live with the Hayeses in a rental apartment a short distance from the labs. Cathy worked to clarify elements of human psychology by examining them from different perspectives. (HSOP.)

By studying Viki in her own home, Cathy could draw comparisons between chimp and human characteristics and between Viki and other chimpanzees at the laboratories. She worked extensively in trying to teach Viki human speech. It was the most successful study of this kind ever, as Viki could say, "Mama," "Papa," and "cup." In the end, the conclusion was that it was not possible for chimps to use human speech. (HSOP.)

Cathy's charming book *The Ape in Our House*, published in 1951, details their project. The little chimp took on many human ways. Viki liked to dial the three digits needed for local calls and, when someone answered, would say, "Boo!" This gave the locals something to talk about at their next visit to the town's post office. "The monkey called me today" was understood by all. (HSOP.)

The Hayeses' apartment was located in the old Clarke Pecan Grove. Carrie Clarke loved the little chimp who could use the rotary telephone. Viki became famous when *Life* magazine came to Orange Park to do a spread on the "Chimp That Can Talk." Published on December 3, 1951, it included many pictures of the Hayeses interacting in middle-class family fashion with Viki. (HSOP.)

Drivers on Kingsley Avenue might have seen Viki swinging through the old Pecan Grove with laundry from the clothesline. She was given some freedom, but fencing was added for her own safety. Her antics delighted local children and inspired the movie *Bedtime for Bonzo*, which starred Ronald Reagan; it was a hit in 1951. Sadly, Viki died three years after the film debuted, a victim of encephalitis. (HSOP.)

In 1953, the Karl Spencer Lashley Award for Distinguished Achievement in the Neurosciences was established in honor of the station's director. At that time, the research station had 12 buildings: a garage, a pumphouse, various sheds, an administration building (shown here), animal quarters, a superintendent's office, a spider monkey house, outdoor cages, and heated shelters. (HSOP.)

The year 1956 was difficult for the station. Henry Nissen, who had married Cathy Hayes following her divorce from Keith, took his own life. Cathy, expecting at the time what would be her only child, resigned and moved to Chicago. An interim director was chosen, but operations were strained. It was decided that Emory University in Atlanta would take over the direction of the Monkey Farm. (Emory University Stuart A. Rose Manuscript, Archives & Rare Book Library.)

Throughout the years the laboratories were in Orange Park, they remained a secret sensation. The close-knit scientific community was well aware of the projects being conducted. The townspeople of Orange Park were unaware of the scope of their achievements. They were happy to receive the extra employment opportunities and left it at that. (Emory University Stuart A. Rose Manuscript, Archives & Rare Book Library.)

New scientists joined the staff for short terms but left due to heat, bugs, and limited intellectual outlets. Among later studies conducted were projects involving brain surgery and others testing radiation exposure in cooperation with the Atomic Energy Commission. The last two directors for the Orange Park plant were Arthur Riopelle and Geoffrey Bourne. (Emory University Stuart A. Rose Manuscript, Archives & Rare Book Library.)

A booming population was beginning to create more demands on the land around the laboratories. Riopelle reported to Ada Yerkes that the town was "growing like kudzu." Privacy could not be maintained. Hurricane Dora, one of the worse in the area's history, took its toll in 1964. It was time for a change. (HSOP.)

Orange Park's Monkey Farm was once the largest center for primate research in the world. The animals were not used for space missions or interspecies breeding, as rumors report. Scientific journals praise the great work done there. Because of the studies done in Orange Park, more is known about chimpanzees than any other animal except white rats. (Emory University Stuart A. Rose Manuscript, Archives & Rare Book Library.)

The structures built for the Monkey Farm still stand. They are in use as office space and retail businesses. There are still remnants of the fencing and cages, though few, unaware of its story, realize why they are there. Efforts are currently underway to place a state historical marker on the site so that the public can appreciate the scope of the story. (Emory University Stuart A. Rose Manuscript, Archives & Rare Book Library.)

The station moved with great fanfare in 1965 to Emory University in Atlanta, where it is now called Yerkes National Primate Research Center. Director Bourne moved with the animals to Atlanta. It works in partnership with the National Institutes of Health and other agencies to create vaccines and probe the causes of and treatment for brain maladies. (HSOP.)

Seven

MOOSEHAVEN

In 1922, the Loyal Order of Moose came to Orange Park to create a "City of Contentment," which was later called Moosehaven. The Moose needed a place for their elderly fraternity members and their spouses to spend the latter years of their lives. Starting in 1918, the Moose scouted many locations before settling on Orange Park. In 1921, the group purchased the old Hotel Marion and eight acres of land. (SAF.)

On October 3, 1922, Moosehaven was officially dedicated. By then, there were 21 residents living in the old hotel, renamed Brandon Hall in honor of the Moose supreme secretary Rodney H. Brandon, who had arranged its purchase. By the end of that year, the land had grown to 26 acres and included several cottages. New residents planted gardens and raised chickens. In 1924, a cooperative farm was established. (CCA.)

In 1924, Orange Park was struggling to bring electricity and phone services to town. This was a project of the Woman's Club and other local citizens. In order to qualify for the service, a minimum number of subscribers was required. Moosehaven, with its growth, had the numbers needed. It guaranteed one half of the pre-subscriptions required to bring the services from Jacksonville. (CCA.)

On July 13, 1927, the Moose, needing more accommodations, bought three old dormitory buildings that had been part of the Orange Park Normal School complex. The organization applied a cobblestone covering to all the structures. By this time, there were around 150 Moose living in Orange Park, performing all their own work and operating a successful dairy and farm. (Mary Jo McTammany.)

By 1930, more buildings dotted the Moosehaven grounds, including a commissary, shoe shop, laundry, and workshop. Growth continued even during the Great Depression. Two rooms inside Brandon Hall served as a hospital until growing need led to a freestanding hospital annex. Before there was another, Moosehaven's doctor served the townspeople. In the 1960s, the $2-million Paul P. Schmitz Health Center was built to meet the needs of Moosehaven residents. (CCA.)

WATER TANK
110ft. High   60,000 Gal.
Moosehaven - Orange Park, Fla.

In 1933, the Philadelphia Building was added for several purposes. Among those was an area functioning through the Women of the Moose where new residents could join a sewing circle and become more comfortable in the community. All this prosperity in the midst of so much need set nerves on end with local residents. Moosehaven, as a charitable institution, was tax-exempt. That too bothered local taxpayers. (CCA.)

By 1940, the economic climate of the country and Moosehaven were changing. The introduction of the Social Security system led to the reconsideration of financial arrangements. Residents were no longer admitted on a "pay" basis. Over half the residents were now in need of medical care, which would require hiring more staff. A system was begun in which retirees turn over everything they own when joining and are guaranteed lifetime care. (CCA.)

Orange Park residents, fewer in number than their elderly Moose neighbors, became alarmed when a postcard was issued from "Moosehaven, Florida." Panic started at the prospect that the town's name might be replaced. Conflicts grew even worse after World War II, because local land prices were rising at alarming rates, and Moosehaven, by 1949, had over $2 million invested in Orange Park's best land. (SAF.)

Town commissioners sued Moosehaven for taxes in spite of its charity status. The dispute was settled out of court, with Moosehaven agreeing to donate $1,000 per year to the town in place of taxes. It also agreed that its residents wouldn't be part of local elections. Additionally, when it built a new complex for itself, it gave the town part of the original normal school buildings it had bought in 1927. (CCA.)

By the 1960s, most of the people of Orange Park saw the Moose as an integral part of their community. The grounds of Moosehaven became useful for residents once the farming initiative changed for the retired Moose. The first attempt at organized baseball for boys in Orange Park was played on the open grounds that had once been farmed fields. (SAF.)

Outdoor Shuffleboard Courts, Moosehaven, Florida

Residents once raised crops and chickens but now enjoy an easier life at Moosehaven. They spend time pursuing hobbies or helping with "Sunshine Jobs," such as answering phones, delivering mail, or other easy jobs. The grounds of Moosehaven are open to the public on a fairly regular basis with community breakfasts, chili cook-offs, and holiday gatherings that mix the elderly residents with the community at large. (CCA.)

Eight

BUILDING COMMUNITY

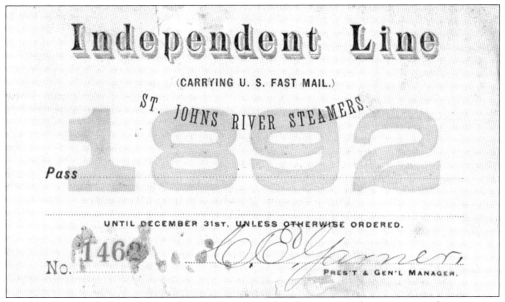

In spite of originally being built to be a tugboat, the *May Garner* steamboat was a regular transport for freight and passengers of Orange Park. With regular stops at Green Cove Springs, Jacksonville, Mandarin, and Orange Park, the steamboat was a communication and logistical link that helped the community grow and thrive. Recreational uses included day trips into Mandarin for picnics, hunting, and relaxation. (HSOP.)

In the 1880s, Burdette Jay "B.J." Johnson, founder of Johnson's Soap Company, brought his family to Orange Park for the winter. He had already lost two children to consumption when his daughter Karrie contracted the disease. The winters in his Milwaukee home were harsh, so Johnson came to Florida to save his daughter. The family stayed at the Park View House, and Karrie recovered her health in Florida's sunshine. (CCA.)

B.J. Johnson soon rented a house across the street from the hotel. The house, built in 1874, was expanded and became the winter home of the Johnson family for many years. Karrie Johnson survived and grew to love Orange Park. As an adult, she persuaded her husband, John Albert Ferguson, to buy the waterfront home and its surrounding land. Remembering the winters of her youth, they named their property Winterbourne. (CCA.)

The B.J. Johnson family helped turn the town into a community. Johnson knew Washington Benedict before coming to Orange Park, and together, they supplied oak trees to line Kingsley Avenue, defining it as a road long before pavement was added. Johnson thus led the way for future generations of his family who beautified the town with gardens and green spaces, a pattern that continues today. (HSOP.)

Approaching Winterbourne from Kingsley Avenue, one would pass servants' quarters and a garage lined against a row of oaks. There were no paved streets, sewer, water, or electricity services. Maintaining a large property required lots of paid help, which created jobs in the town. In 1917, Karrie Ferguson sold 20 acres of her land to her brother, Caleb, who was retiring from the Palmolive Soap Company. (CCA.)

By 1883, Orange Park had telegraph and railroad services. Work was available requiring various levels of education. There were stores, churches, factories, and a school. Farms produced citrus, strawberries, and vegetables that were shipped by steamboat or railroad. All local governance was conducted on a volunteer basis. Local people organized themselves to provide additional services. (CCA.)

Caleb and his wife, Elinor, built a Mediterranean Revival luxury estate named Mira Rio near Winterbourne in 1922. It included an artesian well to charge an electric turbine that lit the house. There was an extensive staff, including a butler, maids, a chauffeur, and groundskeepers. To keep everyone fed required hundreds of chickens, two cows, and a large vegetable garden. (CCA.)

In 1912, William and Carrie Clarke (second from left) built a home on a 30-acre farm tract off Kingsley Avenue. William (third from left), a plumber from Jacksonville, wanted his only child, Bill (far left), to have a rural childhood. In 1909, while keeping the plumbing business going, he started farming fruit on his Orange Park land, switching later to pecans, which were more freeze tolerant. (HSOP.)

Clarke Pecan Grove was on the cutting edge of the newly viable pecan industry. William Clarke took a scientific approach to cultivation that was very successful. His compost was described in the *Nut-Growers* agricultural journal in 1919, explaining he combined fish heads, leaf mold, and manure of various animals. The property raised cows, chickens, and goats. With the help of Robert Jacobs (pictured), it was a multifunctional farm. (HSOP.)

William Clarke commuted daily to his Jacksonville plumbing business by automobile. The road to town went along the river in Orange Park into Duval County, through the remains of Mulberry Grove Plantation, and past the National Guard's Camp Johnson. It was a long trip, and the road turned sandy or muddy depending on the weather. The only other way to work would have been by steamboat. (HSOP.)

The Clarkes were generous public servants. William was a valuable member of the town commission and served as mayor. Carrie Clarke started the First Baptist Church Sunday school on her front porch in 1921. She had acquired land for the church's first sanctuary (pictured) at a county bankruptcy sale for $1. The Clarkes opened their home to any couples needing a wedding venue and fed hungry neighbors during the Great Depression. (HSOP.)

In 1921, going to Orange Park's school on McIntosh Avenue could be a matter of whose turn it was to ride the pony. Pictured here are children of the Montgomery, Horton, Houston, Blitch, Strom, and Harvey families. This pony was referred to as "our faithful friend." The school (see page 94), like so many in town, served multiple purposes. (Mary Jo McTammany.)

The center of small-town community life for many years was the post office. It was a place one could go and expect to run into neighbors, a place to exchange news and gossip, and a place that linked the town with the world at large. The town's first post offices were in stores, generating guaranteed traffic. As the town grew, that became less practical. (HSOP.)

After William Clarke's death in 1943, the Pecan Grove closed. The buildings where workers lived on the property were converted into rental apartments to provide income for Carrie Clarke until her death in 1979. One rental structure remains on the property, along with the Clarke House, garage, and storage barn. The town purchased the 15-acre tract in 1991 as a community park for residents and visitors. (HSOP.)

Through the 1920s, the Fergusons of Mira Rio enjoyed parties, bridge, boating, horseback riding, swimming, and even fancy-dress balls. When World War II came, the club offered housing to aviation trainees at local navy bases. The property was temporarily renamed Azaleana Manor during the war years. Joseph Kennedy Jr. and Ed McMahon stayed there while they served at Lee Field in Green Cove Springs. (CCA.)

The Orange Park Woman's Club was the first civic organization in town, founded in 1910 by eight women with a desire to serve their community. With leader Mary Berry, the club adopted Orange Park Elementary as its first project, raising money to buy slates and drinking cups for students. It also purchased trash barrels for the town. Soon after forming, the club cared for 100 people during a malaria outbreak. (CCA.)

In 1911, the Woman's Club established a library that functioned for 50 years. The first librarian, Anna Allen, was thrilled to receive the first donation of 25 books from Alicia Van Buren to start the library. Money was raised to provide lamps and bookcases. During World War I, the Woman's Club arranged for dances and entertainment at Camp Johnston (now Naval Air Station Jacksonville) and began volunteering with the Red Cross. (HSOP.)

Orange Park's celebration of the Fourth of July was arranged, advertised, and run by the Woman's Club in 1922. An all-day affair with boxed lunches, ice cream, lemonade, and games ended with a launch of floating candles on the river. There were athletic competitions and demonstrations. The event was advertised to draw from surrounding communities. (HSOP.)

In 1924, the ladies helped bring electricity to the town. In 1929, the Woman's Club built a clubhouse with land donated by Charles and Margery Brown. The structure began with a donated mail-order "Mitchell" model house from the Sears Roebuck's catalog. The building is listed among the historic structures of the town. (CCA.)

The post office was conveniently located near the sporting goods store in Orange Park's version of a strip mall in the 1920s. At this time, there were about 60 students in the Orange Park School, grades one through nine. A new school was needed, so the Clay County Board of Public Instruction floated a $25,000 bond to start building Orange Park Elementary. (HSOP.)

Orange Park Elementary School was completed in 1928, with classes beginning in January 1929. Until 1946, the school had three teachers, one of whom served as principal. Hot lunches began to be served here in 1932, begun by Anna Allen and continued by the Woman's Club, which also provided clothing and eyeglasses for children in need. (HSOP.)

Hildreth Hall had many uses after the closing of the normal school. The town fathers let the Woman's Club use it as a library, which functioned until after World War II, when the state centralized the library system and built a new branch library. The Lion's Club met there for a time. The building became town offices in 1948, and the town had ample space for the first time. (HSOP.)

The building behind Willa Mae and George Montague was the town's first school and later, in the 1940s, served as the Masonic hall. The Montagues lived down the street for a time and had long lives in Orange Park. George had several different homes in his 94-year lifetime, all of which were within five miles of one another. (Mary Jo McTammany.)

Madeline Moore came to Orange Park in 1950 and, seeing a need in the community, started collecting clothes and food in the trunk of her Nash Rambler. That led to the creation of the Clothes Closet and Food Pantry of Orange Park, which has served the community since 1952. It provides emergency assistance with food, clothing, household, and financial needs in a compassionate manner to families and individuals in Clay County. (HSOP.)

Teresa Miller was a dedicated teacher for 40 years. Here, she is taking her students to the small African American Pear Grove school in the 1950s. She is remembered fondly. The school that is now called Grove Park Elementary was once named for Teresa Miller. At the time of her death in 2003, she was Teresa Miller Caldwell. (Mary Jo McTammany.)

This McIntosh Avenue building was the Orange Park Negro Elementary School, renamed the T.C. Miller Center to honor its teacher. It was a vast improvement over the Pear Grove schoolhouse. Florida's Site File lists its construction date as 1920, but the National Register of Historic Places puts it at 1938. Today, it is a community center owned by the town and hosts the Clay County Youth Character Building Program, providing youth services in the community. (UNF, Thomas G. Carpenter Library, Special Collections and University Archives, George Lansing Taylor Jr. Collection.)

Karrie Johnson Ferguson lived in Winterbourne until her death, well into her 80s. Thirteen years after her 1952 death, the home was sold to Karrie's great-nephew Jon Massee, who converted the property into a private social club called Club Continental. Tennis courts and a yacht basin with 85 slips were added. The complex began its current role as a wedding and party venue as well as a charming inn. (CCA.)

Back in April 1953, Mira Rio hosted a meeting of the town's more affluent families to create a new school in Orange Park. Helen Adams, with Margot (granddaughter of Caleb Johnson) and her husband, Ash Tisdale, brought the town's wealthier families together with Dr. Edwin Heinrich to establish a private school. Orange Park's population had reached 1,500 by that point, and Adams believed the school was needed to relieve local overcrowding. (St. Johns Country Day School.)

Applications for the new St. Johns Country Day School began four months after the meeting. Before a larger campus could be created, the school met in the old normal school buildings. The new campus, located just outside town limits, began construction in 1957 and continued into the 1960s. St. Johns Country Day is still considered part of the Orange Park community. (St. Johns Country Day School.)

This house on the corner of Blake Avenue and River Road functioned as a summer haven for Jacksonville children from an orphanage run through St. Joseph's Parish in Jacksonville. There was an indoor swimming pool for the children and plenty of rural sunshine. The house burned to the ground at a time when there was no one inside. (Mary Jo McTammany.)

During World War II, the Woman's Club helped care for returning wounded soldiers. It sold war bonds and worked with the Red Cross. The club, under the leadership of Mary Ann Study, sponsored the historic building survey for Orange Park that led to the creation of a Florida historic district for River Road between Blake Avenue and Kingsley Avenue East. The club's float, seen here, was to honor the county centennial. (CCA.)

In the 1960s, a new library was added to the area where town hall sits today. This free-standing building replaced the old normal school building and was considered very modern and a sign of prosperity. Later, a newer library was built on Plainfield Avenue, part of the Clay County Library System, and the Friends of the Orange Park Library group started. Cobblestones from the old normal school were used by locals to build homes. (HSOP.)

The Garden Club of Orange Park became a Federated Club on June 1, 1958. Its first project was cleaning up the town, all four corners. Volunteers armed with rakes, spades, and pruning shears cleaned up Kingsley Avenue. Carrie Clarke was among them and donated daylilies to the project. From left to right, Founder's Circle volunteers Faye Irvin, Carol McConnell, Jean Lyon, and Dot Patterson work in Clarke Park. (HSOP.)

The Rotary Club of Orange Park, chartered on September 17, 1969, develops community service projects that address issues of children at risk, poverty and hunger, the environment, illiteracy, and veterans' needs. In 2004, the club dedicated a veterans memorial at Moosehaven. The Rotary motto is "Service above self, they profit most who serve best." The Rotary Pavilion at Moosehaven serves in many ways. (HSOP.)

In 1993, the Garden Club bought a small place at 1820 Smith Street and a portable building from St. Luke's Catholic Church, which was moved to the same site. It continues to improve green spaces around the town and maintain small gardens in public places. Partnering with other nonprofits, the club also creates lovely centerpieces for special occasions. (HSOP.)

The Town of Orange Park liked the results of the Garden Club's actions and let it use a house on Smith Street for a few years. The club installed a Blue Star marker on Highway 17 in 1969 to honor America's veterans. It was moved in 2011 to the site of the Veterans Memorial in Orange Park's Magnolia Cemetery, where it would receive more notice. (Orange Park Garden Club.)

In 1970, the Orange Park Woman's Club established a day camp for handicapped children. In 1974, the club started the Hospital Auxiliary for the new Orange Park Medical Center. When the historic Clarke House was acquired by the town in 2003, the members staged a fundraiser fashion show to fix it up. They donated a pavilion in 2012 (seen here). The club today runs a thrift shop to provide income for scholarship programs. (HSOP.)

Art Guild of Orange Park, Inc., was established in 1973 to promote the fine visual arts in Clay County and northeast Florida. The guild provides ongoing opportunities for the development and enrichment of artist members. It also sponsors youth programs and a scholarship program to encourage artistic development in local students. There is often a display of art guild works on the walls of town hall's lobby. (HSOP.)

Club Continental thrived in the 1960s under Caleb "Jon" Massee's leadership. Jon's wife, Frederica "Frica" McIntosh Massee, led a community effort to preserve historic buildings in Clay County. She fell in love with the old Fleming Plantation property south of town and, in 1976, rescued its 1860s-era golf course clubhouse from demolition. She restored the house, and today, it is a pub called the River House. (HSOP.)

In 1998, local historian Mary Ann Study worked tirelessly with members of the Orange Park Woman's Club to create a historic district. Ten structures that front onto River Road and Stiles Avenue were included. Six of them were on River Road and were built between 1912 and 1925. Two on Stiles Avenue, including the DeMarco home (built in 1926), also had an outbuilding listed, accounting for the total of 10 structures. (HSOP.)

The Art Guild of Orange Park works with other organizations to achieve common goals in various fields. In 2008, Carolyn Day, as leader of the guild, created a coloring book for kids celebrating Clay County's 150th anniversary. The guild members designed pages representing historic structures in the town. They also conducted a student art contest for the design of the coloring book cover and sent copies to local elementary schools. (HSOP.)

In 2010, Carolyn Ann Day listened to a war bride talk about creating a veterans memorial in Keystone Heights, Florida. Using her artistic talents, she sketched out a design for an Orange Park version. That spark and years of hard work have given Orange Park a beautiful memorial to honor the town's veterans. This was sponsored by the Town of Orange Park, the Sofia Fleming Chapter of the Daughters of the American Revolution, and the American Legion Riders Post No. 250. Inscribed on bricks in front of the memorial are the names of veterans who have some connection to Orange Park's citizens. Also engraved on bricks are the names of all of Clay County's killed-in-action since the town was created. The Historical Society of Orange Park conducts a Veterans Day ceremony each year at the site attended by hundreds. (HSOP.)

In 2015, St. Catherine's Catholic Church overflowed as the town turned out to mourn the death of Mary Helen Hoff. Mary came to Orange Park in 1969 with her husband, Navy commander Michael Hoff. In 1970, during deployment to Vietnam, Michael was declared missing in action. This mother of five became an activist for POW/MIAs and helped create the flag so recognized today. She exemplified faithful service. (HSOP.)

The ladies of the Sofia Fleming Chapter of the Daughters of the American Revolution (DAR) are dedicated to education, historical preservation, and patriotism. In 2011, these local ladies filed paperwork with the national DAR to receive financial support vitally needed to make the historical society's veterans memorial project happen. Their ongoing patriotic efforts and continued participation in the annual Veterans Day celebrations at the memorial are assets to the community. (HSOP.)

Nine

SMALL-TOWN PLEASURES

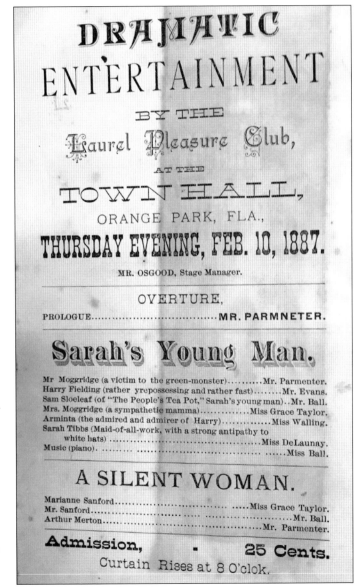

Entertainment in the 1880s was left to the creativity of early residents. William Parmenter, along with friends and family, helped fill the void. Little plays were performed in town hall for the admission price of 25¢. The Parmenter family saved mementos from the shows, compiling them into scrapbooks later donated to the Florida Archives. (HSOP.)

By 1906, pleasurable day trips were made by steamboat or taxi. The cab seen here made stops between Jacksonville, Orange Park, Magnolia, and Green Cove Springs. A nonstop excursion to swim in the springs or visit extended family took just over one hour from Orange Park. Similarly, folks from Green Cove Springs could come for a day trip to Orange Park to enjoy the Magnetic Roaring Springs. (Clay County Historical Society.)

Small-town celebrations would not be complete without Boy Scouts and patriotic decorations. Here, in 1929, a crowd begins to gather for a parade to go down Kingsley Avenue. The men pictured are, from left to right, George Shumeyer, George Austead, and Carl Elmore. This time period marked the start of the decline in naval stores operations in the town and the county. The trees continued to provide, but other occupations were needed. (SAF.)

Orange Park citizens wanted a United Methodist church inside the town limits. A congregation of about 10 people started meeting in the old town hall, but conditions were not good. The congregation had also started to outgrow the space. So, in 1947, when Camp Blanding started selling off its wartime buildings, a group of people acted fast. It bought the camp's hospital building and transported it to Orange Park. (CCA.)

The new Methodist congregation held fish-fry dinners to finance remodeling. Later, when it was able to buy the base chapel from Camp Blanding, the whole community turned out to watch it being moved into place. The old structure was demolished, and the new one stood in its place for the next 45 years. In 1993, a bigger building was constructed, and the old chapel was moved again to serve elsewhere. (CCA.)

The Shepherd's Center of Orange Park offers programs for seniors to socialize through dances, parties, picnics, barbecues, and other activities. The center, started in 1993, sponsors a Golden Years Gala event annually to recognize seniors in six different categories. The 2012 winner (center with Ken Amaro and Cindy Stewart) was Dr. Virginia Hash, "the Science Lady" of Doctor's Inlet Elementary. (HSOP.)

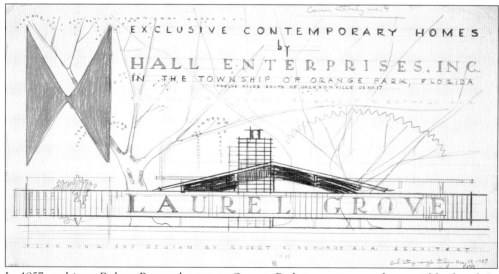

In 1957, architect Robert Broward came to Orange Park to create a modern neighborhood. In all, he was able to design 14 homes before problems set in to stop any additional. Broward was known for incorporating nature into design, using the natural elements of the environment to determine style and form. His Laurel Grove community in Orange Park offered such charm as well as maximum privacy. (University of Florida, George A. Smathers Libraries.)

In the 1950s, when a group of Orange Park boys wanted to play baseball, they could go to the open area of Moosehaven. By the 1960s, there were just too many kids in town for that. In March 1962, Robert Griffin offered to sell some of his land to make a ballpark. After a little bargaining, the town agreed to buy six and a half acres for $2,850. (HSOP.)

Getting the land surveyed and ready took too long. In April 1963, the first Little League games started at Orange Park Elementary's field instead. Robert Griffin made another offer to the town for more of his land. Meanwhile, an Orange Park Little League Board of Directors was assembled for competitive baseball. The directors were Buck Murphy, Bob Nolan, Barney Clark, and Dick Fromhart. (HSOP.)

The Orange Park Athletic Association (OPAA) was launched on May 3, 1963, at a dedication ceremony hosted by Glenn Alred of the Lion's Club, Mayor Walter Odom, Rev. Gene McCullough of the First Baptist Church, and Bob Nolan, town manager and coach. A constitution and bylaws were adopted. The driving force behind all this was Dick Fromhart, for whom a street would later be named. (HSOP.)

Finally, in December 1965, the OPAA purchased the land west of Fromhart Street from Griffin. Land and service negotiations went back and forth for another year. In December 1966, the town council agreed to a 10-year lease with Little League of Orange Park, Inc. However, some games were still played at Orange Park Elementary. (OPAA.)

Games started being played on the Fromhart property in 1968. The OPAA started with two fields and one concrete building in which to store gear. Originally, baseball was played in spring and football in winter. They were played on the same fields at first. John Davis and Dick Shipley are responsible for getting the football teams playing. By 1969, four softball teams were added to the mix. (TOP.)

The athletic association drew a lot of attention. A concession stand was added; it was considered a very big deal at the time. A swimming pool was added to the site but had a lot of problems, so after a while, it was filled in, and that area remains vacant. OPAA remains a vital presence in Orange Park. The town has added a playground (called Gano Park) and other features. (TOP.)

In 2002, OPAA dedicated a new football field to Dick Shipley (seen here) for his 30 years of dedication. Shipley was "Coach" to generations. Similarly, a field was named to honor John Davis, who also gave three decades of devotion. The 1987 Cyclones, coached by John Davis and Dick Shipley, won the Pop Warner Conference title—something no other Orange Park team did for the next 14 years. (OPAA.)

The last addition to Fromhart Street's public amenities was Orange Park Skate Park (constructed in 2000), which is owned by the town but managed by a group of volunteers called Orange Park Patrons. The skate park offers youth a free alternative for recreation within a clean, well-run facility. There is a pro shop, concessions, playground, and safety supervision. For years, Anjie Palmer has been the driving force in this wonderful public park. (TOP.)

Vietnam POW and later Sen. John McCain (bottom right) was stationed at Naval Air Station Jacksonville before being deployed. For over five years, his family lived in Orange Park's new neighborhood designed by architect Robert Broward while McCain was a POW. His wife taught at Orange Park Elementary, where his children were students. His hero's welcome home included the town and full student body of Orange Park Elementary. (Library of Congress.)

Since 1981, the town has presented Memorial Day ceremonies each year at the Veterans Memorial site inside Magnolia Cemetery. These events are overseen by the fire department with funding from the generosity of Gloria Hackett. It was her way of remembering her late husband, Felix. Since Hackett's death in 2010, the ceremonies continue due to a bequest she made for that purpose. (HSOP.)

In 1995, Orange Park mayor Earl Harrington presented the plaque and time capsule installed in the new town hall building under construction. Harrington served many years on the town council and was mayor five times, the most of any individual. A lifetime resident of Orange Park, he started its American Pie Fourth of July Celebration, which was held for years, and was a charter member of the Historical Society of Orange Park. (HSOP.)

In 1981, Orange Park was designated a tree and bird sanctuary, requiring the town to protect nature. Each year, the town holds an Arbor Day celebration like the one shown here in 2004. Participants include Mayor Steve Jones (far left); Helen Howard of the Garden Club, above the flag's tree; Carolyn Clark, representing the historical society, to the left of Howard; and Ernest Jones, parks superintendent (in white cap). (HSOP.)

Since 2004, in recognition of Carrie Clarke, an annual celebration is held every March at Clarke Park. Carrie's altruism was a natural part of who she was. She helped in the development of a lot of local groups that address issues for the greater good. These include the First Baptist Church, the Garden Club, and the Woman's Club. She was known for kind works and neighborly kindness. (HSOP.)

Over the years, from left to right, Barney Clark, Art Hall, and Bill Jackson have demonstrated old-fashioned laundry techniques to thousands of Clarke Day visitors. Jackson also explains how he makes his own soap. Hall explains water gathering methods, and Clark adds humor to demonstrations, all outside the Clarkes' pecan shed. The Clarkes boiled wash water using fire from the chimney here. (HSOP.)

Clarke Day is a chance for local nonprofits to set up tables to share their goals and let the public know what services they provide. It is a chance for old-fashioned picnics on the grounds and homegrown music. There have been games, competitions, and home-baked goodies at every Carrie Clarke Day. It is a wonderful chance to reflect on the contributions of the town's founders and friends. (HSOP.)

The large Clarke Park playground started with Hank Racer, who, in 1998, approached the parks and recreation committee with ideas to construct a community playground. He then led an ad hoc committee to explore the idea. The state would help fund the purchase of the parkland through sales tax revenues. About that time, the Clarke property on Kingsley Avenue was put up for sale. (TOP.)

The town purchased Clarke Park, and Hank Racer formed a nonprofit corporation called Project Playground. With dedicated volunteers, he then raised over $150,000 for the construction funds and recruited people to construct the playground. Volunteers constructed the playground in about one week in early 2000. It was the largest public playground in the state of Florida at that time. (HSOP.)

Each year since 1982, the town of Orange Park holds an annual fall festival. It is considered Clay County's oldest and largest arts and crafts festival, starting with barely a dozen booths and a few musicians. Now, the two-day festival has over 200 booths and two stages with entertainment. There are activities for kids, farm goods, vendors from around the Southeast, live music, and booths for nonprofits of all kinds. (TOP.)

In 2012, the town introduced Reel Fun Nights, shown here, to the community. A large outdoor screen was placed in the town hall park, and families brought lawn chairs to watch the movie together. Moosehaven popped popcorn and provided the sound system needed. The event included rides before the movie started and was a big success. Several such nights are offered annually. (TOP.)

In 2011, the Historical Society of Orange Park proposed a Christmas celebration be held inside Clarke Park to bring the community together for old-fashioned fun. The society couldn't afford to advertise, so the town volunteered to help, and Hometown Holiday is now an annual success. Today, traditions are shared alongside modern fun. Here, James Wisehart learns to make garland with cranberries. (TOP.)

At Hometown Holiday, the town provides thousands of lights throughout Clarke Park and hayrides through the wooded winter wonderland. There are vendors, games, and even snow (artificial, of course). The society gives Clarke House tours and stations historical character actors around the park to tell visitors about life in old Orange Park. Students fill Past-Ports with signatures as though traveling to faraway places. (TOP.)

Every year, the town displays special decorations and lights. This tradition dates back decades. For many, these signal the start of the holiday season. Also, early in December, the fire department organizes a light parade that brings Santa Claus all throughout neighborhoods within the town to ring in the holiday season. (TOP.)

In 2003, young Chris Louviere adopted the Clarke House porch as his Eagle Scout project. He painted and repaired the porch and its screens so that the community would be able to enjoy the porch as the Clarke family had done. When the project was complete, he presented the process in a program for the historical society. (HSOP.)

The Orange Park Farmers' and Arts Market, run by the town's events and recreation division, was created in 2012. The community can come together on these Sundays for arts and crafts by local artists or to buy fresh produce from area farmers. There is also entertainment offered and activities for children. (TOP.)

The historical society, along with the Clay County Historic Preservation Board and the Board of Clay County Commissioners, presented Orange Park with a Florida historical marker in 2014, installed in front of the town hall. This was the first of its kind for Orange Park, unveiled with a ceremony that included county, state, and local representatives. It was not the last such sign to be created, however. (HSOP.)

Prior to the installation of this marker, Orange Park was the only community in Clay County, Florida, not recognized with such a distinction. The marker's placement in Town Hall Park also marks the historical significance this main intersection has earned over the years. It continues to be the center of community life, local political debate, and celebrations great and small. (HSOP.)

ORANGE PARK

Orange Park was the site of a cotton and citrus British plantation. *Laurel Grove*, which was established by William and Rebecca Pengree during Florida's British Period (1763-1783). Following the American Revolution, Florida was returned to Spain, and the Pengrees left. They returned in 1786 with their slaves and a Spanish land grant to produce pine pitch and turpentine (naval stores) for the Spanish. After William's death in 1793, Rebecca ran the plantation until she sold it in 1803 to Zephaniah Kingsley who expanded it. The plantation flourished until it was burned in 1813.

In 1877, the Florida Winter Home and Improvement Company created the Town of Orange Park on most of the original Pengree land claim. Developer Washington Gano Benedict attracted northern buyers by planting acres of oranges in a system of home and agricultural plots. A 5-acre plot sold for $600 and included cleared, fenced land planted with 250 orange trees. River boats brought tourists to the Hotel Marion, including Ulysses S. Grant and Philip H. Sheridan, as well as Buffalo Bill Cody and Chief Sitting Bull in 1880. Small farms, sawmills, and naval stores, in addition to tourism, made up the town's economy.

A FLORIDA HERITAGE SITE
SPONSORED BY THE CLAY COUNTY HISTORIC PRESERVATION BOARD
AND THE FLORIDA DEPARTMENT OF STATE
F-798   2013

On February 19, 2018, a Florida historical marker was dedicated in front of town hall to recognize the Orange Park Normal School. In a joint effort of the town, historical society, and citizens, over 100 people gathered to remember the school and the struggle for equality. Orange Park Junior High students shared essays they wrote about civil rights activists and pulled the large cloth away to reveal the marker. (HSOP.)

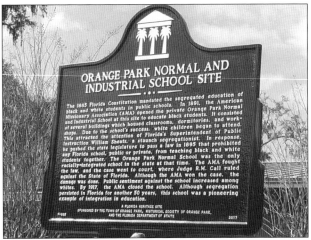

The Historical Society of Orange Park continues to tell the stories of old Florida. The town embraces its history and understands that memories and education enrich and guide our future as we remember our past. The lessons of our founding families teach us to persevere and that working together, this place can nourish us all. (HSOP.)

In 2017, Ernest Jones retired from the town, wrapping up 42 years of service to the community. Here, in 2014, Jones is the first to receive the Earl Harrington Community Service Award. The recognition highlights the painstaking efforts to care for the town's parks and properties, including the historic Clarke House. With Jones is Carol Harrington Hogan, Earl's sister. (HSOP.)

INDEX

ABOUT THE HISTORICAL SOCIETY OF ORANGE PARK

The Historical Society of Orange Park is a 501(c)(3) nonprofit organized to educate the community about the rich and dynamic history of Orange Park, Florida. The society collects, preserves, and displays printed materials of historical value and facilitates educational and historical events.

Through a partnership with the Town of Orange Park and organizations highlighted in this book, the history of Orange Park is being shared. Preserving the story of the Clarke family and their Pecan Grove is important to the town and to the state. The Clarke House, a centerpiece of local history, still has some of its original outbuildings. Efforts are now underway to save the last remaining unpreserved structure. That small green house was used as housing for Pecan Grove workers. The understory of this structure is lined in concrete and was once used to store Clarke's pecans.

Any author royalties earned through sales of this book will be used for local preservation projects, starting with the little green house. Members of the society share Orange Park's history in a variety of ways using the buildings described. The society is very grateful for all the town has done to help it be an agent for the public good in Orange Park.

DISCOVER THOUSANDS OF LOCAL HISTORY BOOKS
FEATURING MILLIONS OF VINTAGE IMAGES

Arcadia Publishing, the leading local history publisher in the United States, is committed to making history accessible and meaningful through publishing books that celebrate and preserve the heritage of America's people and places.

Find more books like this at
www.arcadiapublishing.com

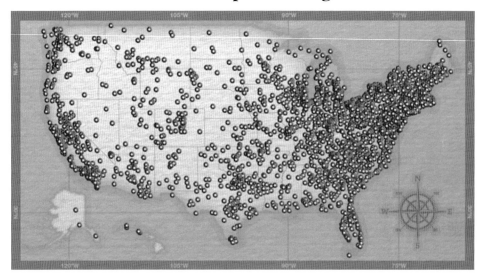

Search for your hometown history, your old stomping grounds, and even your favorite sports team.